MW01098752

Letters and Sounds

-it, -ip, -in

SCHOOL PUBLISHERS

Photos:
p. 2, © PhotoDisc, Inc.; p. 3, © brandXpictures/PunchStock; p. 4, © PhotoDisc, Inc.; p. 5, © Blend Images/PunchStock; p. 6, © PunchStock; p. 7, © PhotoDisc Inc./ PunchStock; p. 8, © PunchStock.

Printed in China

ISBN-13: 978-0-15-358370-4
ISBN-10: 0-15-358370-3

Ordering Options
ISBN 10: 0-15-358355-X (Grade K Below-Level Collection)
ISBN 13: 978-0-15-358355-1 (Grade K Below-Level Collection)
ISBN 10: 0-15-360623-1 (package of 5)
ISBN 13: 978-0-15-360623-6 (package of 5)

4 5 6 7 8 9 10 0940 15 14 13 12 11 10 09

pit

rip

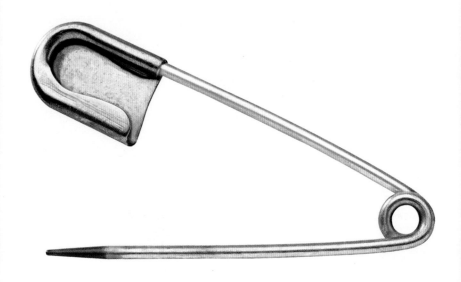

pin

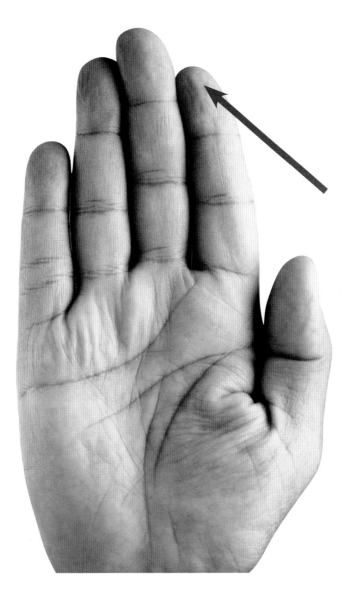

tip

sit

fin

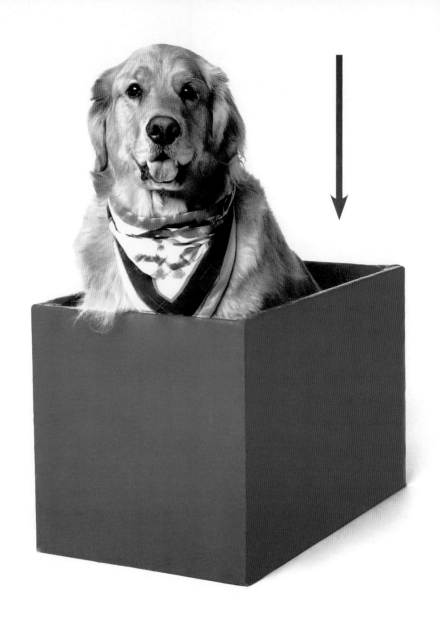

in